GARDEN TO TABLE

NATURE'S MAKERS

JULIE KNUTSON

![Cherry Lake Publishing logo]

Published in the United States of America by Cherry Lake Publishing
Ann Arbor, Michigan
www.cherrylakepublishing.com

Content Advisors: Tim Redmond, owner, Skinny Farm of Scio

Photo Credits: © Christine Cabrera, cover, 1, 8, 15, 22; © Kati Finell/Shutterstock.com, 5; © Tyler Rudick, 6; © Everett Historical/Shutterstock.com, 10; © Julie Knutson, 13, 28; © Courtesy of Tim Redmon, 14, 26; © Lisa Waterman Gray/Shutterstock.com, 16; © Jessie Crow Mermel, 19, 20, 25

Library of Congress Cataloging-in-Publication Data
Names: Knutson, Julie, author. | Knutson, Julie. Nature's makers.
Title: Garden to table / by Julie Knutson.
Description: Ann Arbor : Cherry Lake Publishing, 2019. | Series: Nature's makers | Includes bibliographical references and index.
Identifiers: LCCN 2018036616| ISBN 9781534143036 (hardcover) | ISBN 9781534140790 (pdf) | ISBN 9781534139596 (pbk.) | ISBN 9781534141995 (hosted ebook)
Subjects: LCSH: Farm produce—Juvenile literature. | Farms, Small—Juvenile literature.
Classification: LCC S519 .K58 2019 | DDC 338.1—dc23
LC record available at https://lccn.loc.gov/2018036616

Cherry Lake Publishing would like to acknowledge the work of The Partnership for 21st Century Learning. Please visit www.p21.org for more information.

Printed in the United States of America
Corporate Graphics

ABOUT THE AUTHOR

Julie Knutson is a former teacher who writes from her home in northern Illinois. Researching these books involved sampling a range of farm products, from local honey to heirloom grains to...farm-fresh ice cream! She's thankful to all those who accompanied her on these culinary excursions—most notably to the young ones: Theo, Will, Alex, Ruby, and Olivia.

TABLE OF CONTENTS

CHAPTER 1

Far Away, Close to Home

When farmer Tim Redmond visits fifth-grade classrooms in Ann Arbor, Michigan, he brings bags and bags of … *spinach!*

Yes, spinach. That leafy, **chlorophyll**-rich stuff that rabbits and squirrels love to munch.

Tim doesn't bring just one type of spinach, he brings two. One batch is fresh big-leaf, **overwintered** greens grown on his farm, Skinny Farm of Scio. The other batch is **imported** greens, traveling as much as 4 weeks to reach the desks of these midwestern kids.

While spinach was first cultivated in the Middle East, its first recorded use comes from China, around the year 650 CE.

WEARY TRAVELERS

Visualizing the average miles U.S. produce travels

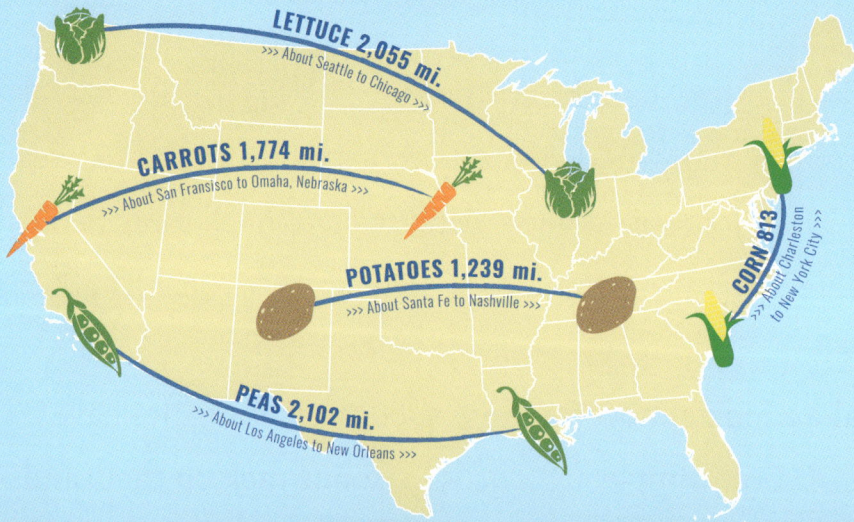

LETTUCE 2,055 mi.
>>> About Seattle to Chicago >>>

CARROTS 1,774 mi.
>>> About San Fransisco to Omaha, Nebraska >>>

CORN 813
>>> About Charleston to New York City >>>

POTATOES 1,239 mi.
>>> About Santa Fe to Nashville >>>

PEAS 2,102 mi.
>>> About Los Angeles to New Orleans >>>

Vegetables can travel a long way to get to your plate.

Tim spears the greens with toothpicks. Then, he asks the students to compare and contrast the flavors. Is there a difference in taste and texture? He savors the moment when the children try his spinach. "Their eyes pop open," he laughs. "And they say, 'Wow, this is really good!'"

What makes Tim's spinach so special? Let's travel to his small farm to learn about how he harvests fruits and vegetables on a small scale.

[21ST CENTURY SKILLS LIBRARY]

Like the store-bought greens that Tim brings to classrooms, many foods journey thousands of miles to your table. Their journey to your plate involves not simply being harvested, but also being processed, boxed, shipped, and shelved.

Take a look at how far these supermarket veggies have traveled. Even simple, unprocessed foods rack up thousands of miles and change many hands to get to your plate.

Corn:	813 miles (1,308 kilometers)
Potatoes:	1,239 miles (1,994 km)
Carrots:	1,774 miles (2,855 km)
Lettuce:	2,055 miles (3,307 km)
Peas:	2,102 miles (3,383 km)

Skinny Farm grows everything from kale to cucumbers to cilantro for more than 40 families, all on a 1.5-acre (0.6 hectares) plot of land.

It all adds up to a lot of distance between producer and consumer, field and fork.

Do all foods crisscross state lines to get to your table? Are there always so many miles, steps, and people between you and your food?

The simple answer is no.

Farms like Skinny Farm of Scio—and farmers like Tim—aim to make it easier for **consumers** to buy local food. Tim harnesses **human capital, physical capital**, and **natural resources** to help customers in and around Ann Arbor, Michigan minimize their food miles.

Will you have a part in Victory?

WRITE TO THE NATIONAL

for free books on gardening, canning & drying.

10

A Garden for Victory!

During World Wars I and II, many citizens of Australia, Canada, England, and the United States picked up their spades and started vegetable gardens. These "victory gardens" were not just in **rural** areas. They were in **suburban** back yards, at schools, and on empty **urban** lots.

What was the reason behind these gardens? It was a time of **rationing**, so growing food for one's own table freed up farm-grown grains and vegetables for overseas troops. It also allowed families to save money.

Backyard farming proved particularly popular during World War II. The most famous was planted on the White House lawn by none other than First Lady Eleanor Roosevelt.

While urban garden patches are often tied to the two wars, their history dates back even earlier. During the Silver Panic of 1893, Detroit mayor Hazen Pingree encouraged backyard farming. The gardeners who worked these plots earned income that helped their families during this **recession**.

CHAPTER 2

The Road to Skinny Farm

Tim didn't grow up on a farm. He was raised in the Detroit, Michigan suburbs in the 1950s and 1960s. He didn't think much about food until he went to college. While a student at the University of Michigan, he became interested in eating more healthfully. He read about it and talked about it with classmates. Eventually, all of this reading and talking led to a business, Eden Foods.

Eden was born out of the belief that Tim and his friends shared that nutritious food should be more easily available. Their mission was to bring wholesome grains, **legumes**, and vegetables to consumers across the country and world.

Tim helped launch Eden Organic in the early 1970s. Today, the products can be found on the shelves of grocery stores and in kitchen pantries nationwide.

Garden plots filled with an array of crops are visible in this aerial view of Skinny Farm.

For the next 40 years, Tim helped build Eden and several other natural foods companies.

In 2008, Tim retired. For the first time in 4 decades, he didn't have to report to work or spend his weeks traveling for business.

Around that same time, a friend of Tim's son named Michael moved back home to Michigan. For years, Michael had worked on organic farms and with agricultural education

[21ST CENTURY SKILLS LIBRARY]

Tim believes local and responsible farming is important for the environment.

organizations in New England. Now he hoped to start a farm in the Ann Arbor area.

Like all farmers, Michael needed a critical resource: land. He didn't have it—but Tim did. So the two paired up to form Skinny Farm of Scio.

The first year, the duo grew garlic. The next year? A Thanksgiving "bounty box" of vegetables and herbs, which they **marketed** to family and friends through email. The farm continued to expand and offered a **community**

supported agriculture (CSA) subscription in its third year. The two men promoted it by placing flyers in neighborhood mailboxes.

After 5 years, Michael had enough capital to buy his own farm. Today, Tim continues the CSA program at Skinny Farm. He provides produce to **shareholders** and local restaurants.

"Farming is one of the most critical professions for the future. It is so necessary that the land be treated well. We need to learn how to raise food without mining out the soil and wrecking our natural resources."

– Tim Redmond

CHAPTER 3

What It Takes

Beyond sun and water, soil and seeds are the most obvious natural resources needed for any agricultural operation. As Tim's farming partner Michael realized early in his career, buying even a small amount of land can be expensive. For young farmers, getting access to soil can be a major challenge.

Costly physical capital, like tractors, combines, and greenhouses, also pose hurdles to many new farmers.

How do aspiring farmers with limited resources—whether money, land, or equipment—enter the profession?

Greenhouses, like this one at Angelic Organics in Caledonia, IL, are physical resources that help extend the growing season.

Many farms offer educational programs and hands-on experience for children and adults alike.

In recent years, many schools and **nonprofits** have worked to connect young people interested in farming with youth camps, training, and **apprenticeships**. Whether at on-campus organic farms or through organizations like 4-H, Future Farmers of America, or the National Young Farmers Coalition, there is a growing network of support for future farmers.

These programs allow newcomers firsthand experience with the science and practice of agriculture. They also build knowledge around the finances of farming. Participants can use these networks to learn about how to get government grants, how to access small urban plots through cooperative organizations, and how to bring products to market.

First-hand experience is essential for new farmers.

A World of Resources

Tim is an agricultural **entrepreneur**. This means he coordinates a variety of resources (or **inputs**) to make products (or **outputs**).

Natural Resources—Land and Animals: Natural resources are just what they sound like: materials that come directly from nature. These resources exist without human intervention. Some natural resources, like the sun and wind, are **renewable**. Others, like oil and coal, are **nonrenewable**. What natural resources are needed at Skinny Farm?

Human Resources—Labor: Human resources are the "people" aspect of any operation. In Tim's case, it's the knowledge, skills, experience, and abilities that he needs to run the farm and CSA. It also includes any help that he gets from paid and volunteer farmworkers.

Physical Resources—Capital: Physical resources are the things that you need to help operate a business, like machines, tools, buildings, and delivery vehicles. What physical resources does Tim need to maintain the farm?

CHAPTER 4

Getting to Market

Tim's daily routine varies with the seasons. Here's an overview of what a typical year looks like on Skinny Farm:

- *December–February:* These are the coldest and quietest months of the year. Crops go dormant and the ground rests. Tim uses this time to plan for the upcoming season, plotting crop placement and rotation. In late winter, he mixes potting soil and starts seeds in indoor trays. Off the farm, Tim visits classrooms to educate kids on food and sustainability.
- *March:* Indoor seeds begin to mature and planning continues.

In spring, farmers welcome early crops, often of the leafy green variety.

WELCOME! SKINNY FARM 2013

* Garlic either 4 lg / 5 Med / 6 sml.
* Onions - 1 bu.
* Potatoes - 1 bg.
* Scallions - 1 bu.
* Scapes - handful
* Eggplant - 2

* Zukes / Smr Sq - 1 big or 2 small
* Cukes - 1 big or 2 small
* Kale + Chard - 1 bunch * Collards 1 bu.
* Tomatoes INSIDE
* Lettuce - 1 bag
* Baby Carrots
* Okra : 2

HERBS
U-PICK

Monthlies:
To rejar -
+ what isn't right but on list

Shareholders can gather their week's bounty at the farm.

26

- *April and May:* When the snow melts, Tim begins to transfer the indoor plants to the greenhouse. These months are also often used for maintenance work around the farm. In late April and early May, Tim and his crew begin to work the ground and form garden beds.
- *June–November:* These are active months for the CSA. Different crops thrive at different times, which means the fruits and vegetables that are "in season" vary by month.

Tim's CSA provides produce for 40 local families and several Ann Arbor restaurants. In the CSA model, shareholders **subsidize** the farm's growing activities by subscribing at the beginning of the growing season. The fees that members pay to the farmer up front are used to buy seeds, tools, packaging, and other resources.

Tim's customers pick up their shares at Skinny Farm, allowing them the chance to interact with their farmer each week. In coming seasons, he hopes to return to the role of assistant and turn the operation over to an aspiring young farmer.

Many farmers who run small operations use CSAs and markets to connect with their customers.

What does Tim enjoy most about farming? Two things. First, he's always learning new things. "Our knowledge of raising food and understanding soil and the interactions involved in it is changing," he explains. "We are on the cutting edge of developing techniques for growing food in a sustainable way. It's just amazing to me what we don't know."

The other thing he enjoys? Community. Farming gives Tim the chance to know his neighbors. Whether they're shareholders wanting to volunteer on the farm, local kids learning about food sources, or chefs at nearby restaurants, Skinny Farm connects Tim to other Ann Arborites.

After a lifetime in the food industry and a decade as a farmer, Tim hopes that a new generation considers working in small-scale agriculture. It's not easy work and it's not always predictable. But there are a lot of perks, including getting to live, work, and eat as close to home as possible.

The City Garden Model Today: Urban Farms

Remember the victory gardens and urban farms mentioned earlier in the book? That model persists today. From Boston to Berkeley and Detroit to Dallas, once-vacant city lots are now vibrant micro-farms.

These green spaces carry many social, economic, and environmental benefits. Socially, they are places where citizens interact and work together. Economically, they allow residents to grow food and flowers to sell at local markets, to restaurants, and through CSAs. This supports stronger regional food economies and allows more residents to have access to nutritious fruits and vegetables. Environmentally, urban gardens reduce the number of miles that food travels, and they beautify the city landscape.

Taking Informed Action

Reducing Food Waste

Beyond reducing food miles, buying fresh local food helps with another major issue: food waste. Skipping the steps of packaging, processing, shipping, and shelving food means that it's less likely to spoil.

What's the big deal with food waste? Food production is a major drain on natural, human, and physical resources. Each year, Americans throw away anywhere from 30 to 40 percent of the food that they buy. This food requires resources and capital to make, accounting for 10 percent of the U.S. energy budget and 80 percent of freshwater.

How can you lessen food waste at home and school? Here are a few ideas:

1) Buy local! The fewer miles that food travels, the less likely it is to spoil.
2) Eat imperfect food! Just because an apple is bruised doesn't mean it's inedible.
3) Follow the three Rs of recycling: reduce, reuse, and recycle (compost). Only buy the food you need and don't waste leftovers. Food scraps left at the end of a meal or that bruised apple's core can be turned into compost.

To build on number three, your school community can follow the lead of students at Chesterbrook Elementary School in McClean, Virginia. Chesterbrook's sixth grade Eco Team helps sort lunch waste into different bins: recyclables, food to be donated, and garbage. This effort is supported by a local organization called Food Bus, which provides refrigerators to keep perishables like milk, yogurt, and cheese from spoiling. At the end of each week, any food that can be donated is taken to a local food pantry.

The results? Food Bus works with 12 schools, and at the end of the 2013–2014 school year, these schools provided 13,502.6 pounds (6,124.7 kilograms) of food to their local food pantries.

GLOSSARY

apprenticeships (uh-PREN-tis-ships) positions working as assistants to experts to learn new skills or trades

chlorophyll (KLOR-uh-fil) green pigment in all green plants that absorbs light to provide energy for photosynthesis

community supported agriculture (kuh-MYOO-nih-tee suh-POR-tid AG-rih-kuhl-chur) a subscription food delivery service that allows consumers to buy food directly from local farmers

consumers (kuhn-SOO-murz) people who buy a product

entrepreneur (ahn-truh-pruh-NUR) a person who coordinates resources (natural resources, human capital, physical capital) to create a product and make a profit

human capital (HYOO-muhn KAP-ih-tuhl) a person's knowledge and experience that can be used in operating a business

imported (im-POR-tid) brought in or shipped from elsewhere

inputs (IN-puts) factors needed to make a product, such as natural resources, human capital, and physical capital

legumes (LEG-yoomz) plants that are members of the pea family, including beans, chickpeas, and peanuts

marketed (MAHR-kit-ed) promoted and advertised a business or service

natural resources (NACH-ur-uhl REE-sors-iz) materials like land and water that occur in nature that can be used for economic gain

nonprofits (nahn-PRAH-fits) organizations that do not have profit as their goal or driver

nonrenewable (nahn-rih-NOO-uh-buhl) natural resources that can run out, such as oil and coal

outputs (OUT-puts) the amount of goods produced using various inputs in a given period of time

overwintered (oh-vur-WIN-turd) a process of cutting back plants in late fall, allowing their roots to stay in the soil through the winter and produce an early spring crop

physical capital (FIZ-ih-kuhl KAP-ih-tuhl) resources like machines and equipment that people need to run a business

rationing (RASH-uhn-ing) conserving a resource

recession (rih-SESH-uhn) period of economic downturn

renewable (rih-NOO-uh-buhl) natural resources that never run out, like the sun and wind

rural (ROOR-uhl) in the country

shareholders (SHAIR-hohl-durz) owners of shares in a company or organization

subsidize (SUHB-sih-dize) to financially support

suburban (suh-BUR-buhn) the area surrounding a city

urban (UR-buhn) a highly populated area; a city

FURTHER READING

Banyard, Antonia, and Paula Ayer. *Eat Up! An Infographic Exploration of Food.* Toronto: Annick Press, 2017.

Mickelson, Trina. *Free-Range Farming.* Minneapolis: Lerner Publications, 2016.

Pirog, Rich, and Tim Van Pelt. "How Far Do Your Fruit and Vegetables Travel?" *Leopold Letter,* April 2002, ucanr.edu/datastoreFiles/608-319.pdf.

Reeves, Diane Lindsey. *Food & Natural Resources: Exploring Career Pathways.* Ann Arbor, MI: Cherry Lake Publishing, 2017.

Vogel, Julia. *Save the Planet: Local Farms and Sustainable Foods.* Ann Arbor, MI: Cherry Lake Publishing, 2010.

INDEX